Assoc. Prof. Erkan YILDIRIM

Growth

The Quick Cash Code: A Blueprint for Rapid Online Earning

Table Of Contents

Chapter 1: Understanding the Online Earnings Landscape — 4

The Evolution of Online Income Opportunities — 4

Common Misconceptions About Making Money Online — 7

Why Rapid Online Earnings Are Achievable — 11

Chapter 2: Setting the Foundation for Quick Cash Success — 16

Identifying Your Skills and Interests — 16

Choosing the Right Online Platform — 19

Establishing Realistic Goals for Quick Cash Generation — 26

Chapter 3: Strategies for Rapid Online Earnings — 30

Leveraging Afiliate Marketing for Quick Cash — 30

Creating Proitable Digital Products — 36

Monetizing Your Blog or Website for Quick Returns — 43

Chapter 4: Implementing the Quick Cash Code Blueprint — **50**

Developing a Consistent Content Strategy — 50

Building a Strong Online Presence — 52

Engaging with Your Target Audience for Maximum Impact — 56

Chapter 5: Scaling Your Quick Cash Business — **59**

Outsourcing and Automation for Eficiency — 59

Diversifying Your Income Streams — 62

Investing Your Quick Cash Proits for Long-Term Growth — 63

Chapter 6: Overcoming Challenges and Staying Motivated — **66**

Dealing with Setbacks and Failure — 66

Staying Focused on Your Quick Cash Goals — 69

Celebrating Your Successes and Milestones — 70

Chapter 7: The Quick Cash Code Success Stories — **72**

Entrepreneur Success Stories — 72

Stay-at-Home Parent Success Stories — 74

Student Success Stories   76

Side Hustler Success Stories   78

**Chapter 8: Taking Action and Unlocking Your
Quick Cash Potential**   **80**

Creating Your Personal Quick Cash Action
Plan   80

Implementing the Strategies outlined in
the Quick Cash Code Blueprint   83

Continuing to Learn and Adapt for
Ongoing Success   84

**Conclusion: Embracing the Quick Cash
Mindset for Lasting Online Earnings Success**   **87**

Chapter 1: Understanding the Online Earnings Landscape

The Evolution of Online Income Opportunities

In today's fast-paced digital world, the landscape of income opportunities has shifted dramatically. The traditional 9-5 job is no longer the only path to financial success. With the rise of the internet, there are now countless ways to earn money online, from the comfort of your own home.

This subchapter will explore the evolution of online income opportunities and how you can leverage them to achieve rapid online earnings.

The era of depending solely on traditional employment for financial security is fading. Today's dynamic economic landscape calls for a multi-faceted approach to income generation.

A diverse group comprising of visionary entrepreneurs, dedicated stay-at-home parents seeking to contribute to household finances, ambitious students aiming to fund their education, determined side hustlers enhancing their earnings, and savvy individuals on the quest for financial freedom, are all exploring the vast digital universe for financial growth.

The Quick Cash Code emerges as an invaluable guide, providing essential strategies for harnessing a multitude of online revenue channels. It serves not just as an instructional manual but as a strategic roadmap, pinpointing various accessible and profitable paths for income diversification within the digital economy's expanse.

Navigating the digital landscape presents a treasure trove of income-generating avenues, from the flexibility of freelance gigs and the strategic acumen required in online consulting to the bustling world of e-commerce and the lucrative partnerships of affiliate marketing.

This vast expanse of prospects affords you limitless potential to carve out a niche that not only aligns with your personal expertise and passions but also taps into your unique toolkit of abilities. The quest is to pinpoint precisely those areas where your knowledge, talents, and interests converge, and harness these assets to cultivate a diversified portfolio of income streams.

By immersing yourself strategically in the ever-evolving digital economy, you stand to architect an online empire that not only brings in consistent revenue but grows and adapts to the changing tides of online commerce and consumer behavior.

Seize the wealth of online possibilities, and invest in your future by building and nurturing a digital business that can supplement or even surpass traditional income sources.

By doing so, you gradually pave a pathway toward the ultimate prize of financial autonomy, allowing you to dictate the terms of your work-life balance and savor the rewards of a self-styled career.

If your goal is to bolster your existing income, pivot towards an entirely new career path, or to lay the foundations for complete financial autonomy, the Quick Cash Code is an all-encompassing resource designed to equip you with the necessary tools, strategic frameworks, and diverse resources to excel within the dynamic landscape of online income possibilities.

Engaging with this material empowers you to stay ahead of the curve by keeping abreast of evolving trends and emerging technologies, ensuring that you are strategically well-placed to capitalize on the next wave of digital earning potential.

By proactively adapting to market changes and continuously refining your approach based on up-to-date industry knowledge, you are setting the stage to unlock the rapid online earnings you envision, turning your virtual financial dreams into a tangible and prosperous reality.

Common Misconceptions About Making Money Online

The digital realm is often shrouded in myths that, if believed, can impede one's journey to online entrepreneurial triumph. The landscape of internet business is riddled with fallacies and exaggerated tales that can deter aspiring digital moguls.

In this pivotal subchapter, we aim to cut through the noise by dispelling some of the most prevalent and misleading myths surrounding the pursuit of monetary gain on the web.

In this detailed exploration, we'll take apart the common myths and misunderstandings surrounding online money-making, shining a light on the truths of digital entrepreneurship. We aim to eradicate these fallacies by providing you with accurate insights and actionable knowledge, thus clarifying the complexities of earning income online.

By arming you with an unobstructed understanding of the realities and demands of cultivating a prosperous online revenue stream, we establish a solid foundation upon which you can build your imminent success.

Through this process, we'll guide you in transitioning from misconceptions to mastery, outlining the steps and commitments necessary to make significant financial strides within the online market. In doing so, we're not just correcting misconceptions—we're creating a blueprint for you to follow towards lasting achievement in the digital economy.

One of the biggest misconceptions about making money online is that it is easy and requires little to no effort. While it is true that there are many ways to make money online, such as affiliate marketing, dropshipping, or selling digital products, these methods all require hard work, dedication, and consistency. Building a successful online business takes time and effort, just like any other business venture.

The belief that substantial financial resources are a prerequisite for launching an online venture is yet another widespread misunderstanding that needs addressing.

It's true that some initial funding can certainly smooth the path, providing a cushion for marketing or advanced tools.

However, the digital world is brimming with opportunities that require minimal to no financial outlay to begin. Instances abound, such as initiating a blog, which typically demands little more than your time and creativity to share your expertise or passions.

Similarly, constructing an online course can lean on your existing knowledge and affordable or even free platforms to host your content. Additionally, offering freelance services in areas such as writing, graphic design, or programming can be started with just your skills and a simple online presence.

These avenues open the door to entrepreneurial endeavors without the weight of financial burden, empowering you to start small and expand as your online business grows.

The misconception that online earnings are exclusively reserved for the tech-savvy or those with a particular set of specialized skills is widespread, yet it could not be further from the truth. In reality, the digital landscape is an inclusive economic playground where individuals of any background or level of expertise have the opportunity to carve out a profitable niche.

A diverse array of online business ventures is at your fingertips, catering to a multitude of interests and abilities. These opportunities beckon to a broad audience, including dedicated stay-at-home parents seeking supplementary income, diligent students aiming to balance studies with financial stability, those engaged in side hustles looking to diversify their revenue streams, and determined aspiring entrepreneurs ready to embark on a brand-new business journey.

The online world is a bastion of potential for economic advancement; it is not just for the technologically adept, but for anyone with the drive to pursue it.

Dispelling these prevalent misunderstandings is not just an exercise in truth-telling but a powerful means of encouragement. We aspire to instill the confidence necessary for you to embark upon your digital moneymaking journey.

Armed with a clear perspective, steadfast resolve, and the appropriate roadmap, stepping into the world of online income generation becomes less daunting and more achievable.

Armed with the right mindset and determination, along with guidance from those who have successfully navigated the digital marketplace, you possess the capability to access the vast wealth of the digital economy.

The promise of swift online profits and the enticing prospect of financial independence are not mere pipe dreams; they are achievable realities within reach for those who are prepared.

By fostering resilience, a strategic outlook, and an openness to learn from experts in the field, you can bridge the gap between where you stand now and the financial success you aspire to achieve.

The journey toward generating rapid online earnings and achieving a state of financial self-sufficiency begins with the confidence that it is possible and the commitment to make it happen.

As this series progresses, we will explore the intricacies of the Quick Cash Blueprint further, arming you with actionable and effective methods for amassing online wealth, proving that sustainable success in the virtual marketplace is not just a dream, but a very attainable reality.

Why Rapid Online Earnings Are Achievable

In this subchapter, we will explore why rapid online earnings are not only possible but achievable for anyone who is willing to put in the work and follow a proven blueprint for success.

Whether you are an experienced business owner or someone just starting to cultivate their presence in the rich terrain of the digital economy, the online realm presents a vast frontier brimming with opportunities. It offers the potential for rapid and uncomplicated paths to establish various sources of income, each with the capacity to prosper concurrently and complement one another.

For the astute entrepreneur, this digital universe extends an invitation to tap into its seemingly infinite potential, allowing for the creation of diverse and multiple streams of revenue that collectively form a robust financial ecosystem.

These channels, when carefully developed and nurtured, hold the power to sprout into substantial and sustainable forms of wealth. In the fertile landscape of cyberspace, ambition paired with action can lead to thriving digital enterprises.

Armed with the proper mentorship and tactical approaches, you have the capability to harness the robust force of the internet to assemble a lucrative endeavor at an unprecedented pace.

The arena of online business brims with prospects for those whose ambitions span across a variety of goals, from launching a groundbreaking product that disrupts the market to devising a bespoke service that addresses the specific requirements of customers, or developing and selling digital wares such as e-books, instructional courses, or innovative software applications.

The allure of swift online financial rewards resonates throughout the vast digital expanse, signaling that with steadfast persistence and the employment of the right strategies and technology, the realization of your economic expansion ambitions is not a far-fetched dream.

It is indeed possible to witness your entrepreneurial efforts bear fruit with extraordinary rapidity and effectiveness. This promise of accelerated income generation stands as a testament to the power of the digital space to facilitate and amplify business success, making it an ideal platform for the ambitious and the driven to flourish.

Stay-at-home parents frequently seek out opportunities to contribute financially to their household without compromising their responsibilities to family life. The appeal of online income-generating activities lies in their flexibility; these ventures can be undertaken from the tranquility of your own home, meshing seamlessly with your unique schedule and familial obligations.

This ability to earn money online presents a perfect harmony between work and personal life, as it offers the convenience of choosing when and how much to work.

Embraced by many, these virtual avenues for income not only accommodate but also respect the rhythms and routines of family-centric lifestyles, making them an ideal solution for parents striving to balance the dual roles of caregiver and earner.

With the right tools and resources, you can create a successful online business that provides you with the financial freedom you desire.

Students doggedly working to support their educational journeys and side hustlers in search of extra income streams are constantly on the lookout for innovative ways to secure additional finances. The internet, an epicenter of opportunity, teems with a wealth of options for those wishing to quickly monetize their skills or business ideas.

It is a vibrant hub, ripe with a plethora of viable paths to financial gain, each as varied and accessible as the next, catering to the ambitions of a wide array of eager participants.

Whether it's through freelancing, e-commerce, content creation, or countless other digital ventures, the internet offers abundant resources and platforms to accommodate and facilitate the aspirations of any individual hungry for financial enhancement and willing to explore the diverse possibilities it presents.

From undertaking freelance projects in various niches, providing educational guidance via online tutoring platforms, to navigating the burgeoning e-commerce space by selling digital or physical products, the digital domain is a veritable treasure trove.

By strategically aligning with a proven blueprint, one that clearly delineates a route towards swift online financial achievement, enterprising individuals are positioned to witness a significant flow of income with an impressive degree of speed.

These carefully crafted strategies, when implemented effectively, have the capacity to not only shore up bank balances but also to broaden the scope of one's professional life, offering enrichment that extends well beyond the scope of traditional avenues for earning.

This methodical approach to generating revenue online can transform the aspirations of budding entrepreneurs, side hustlers, and anyone keen to monetize their digital presence into a reality that yields both immediate monetary rewards and a more expansive set of professional opportunities and experiences.

For those seeking financial independence, the key to success lies in taking action and implementing a plan that will lead to rapid online earnings. By following the strategies outlined in this book, you can unlock the potential for unlimited income and achieve the financial freedom you desire. With dedication, hard work, and the right mindset, rapid online earnings are well within reach.

Chapter 2: Setting the Foundation for Quick Cash Success

Identifying Your Skills and Interests

To harness the dynamic potential of rapid online earnings, pinpointing your unique skill set and passions is paramount. These elements form the bedrock of your future business, a digital fortress from which you can launch into entrepreneurial success.

Whether you're an entrepreneur, a parent balancing home commitments with the desire to contribute financially, a student navigating academia whilst seeking supplementary income, a professional craving a side endeavor, or an individual on a mission for financial autonomy, awareness of your innate strengths and what genuinely energizes you is the compass that will guide you toward fertile avenues for swift financial gain.

Marrying your innate talents with your passions generates a dynamic synergy that can be a potent catalyst for not only steering you towards more suitable and gratifying income-generating pursuits but also elevating your probability of enduring success and satisfaction within the digital financial domain.

This alignment can serve as a linchpin for unlocking your true potential, as it allows you to channel energy into projects that resonate deeply with your personal and professional ethos.

When your endeavors are fueled by this harmonious combination, you find that motivation flows more naturally, creativity skyrockets, and productivity soars, inevitably leading to more profound achievements and a sense of accomplishment that permeates your online work.

It is this blend of ability and enthusiasm that becomes a driving force, propelling you forward in the competitive yet rewarding landscape of internet entrepreneurship.

Start by taking inventory of your skills. What are you naturally good at? Are you a talented writer, a skilled graphic designer, or a savvy social media marketer? Take note of your strengths and consider how you can leverage them to make money online.

Remember, your skills can be anything from technical abilities to soft skills like communication and problem-solving.

Next, think about your interests. What topics or industries are you passionate about? Do you have a hobby or a niche that you love to explore? By aligning your skills with your interests, you can create a business that not only brings in quick cash but also fulfills you on a personal level.

Remember, recognizing your unique talents and areas of interest should be viewed as a continuous journey of self-discovery. As you accumulate experience and broaden your knowledge base, it's natural for your core competencies and enthusiasms to shift and mature.

This evolution reflects your growth as both an individual and a professional. To fully capitalize on this dynamic process, maintain an openness to venturing into uncharted territories and embrace the willingness to recalibrate your direction in response to new insights.

Being flexible and ready to embrace change is critical for staying relevant and ensuring that your personal and professional paths remain aligned with the most up-to-date version of yourself.

This adaptability is key to seizing novel opportunities that may emerge on the horizon and staying ahead in the fluid landscape of career and self-development.

By taking the time to identify your skills and interests, you will be better equipped to choose the right path to rapid online earnings. Remember, success often comes from doing what you love and leveraging your natural abilities. So, take the time to reflect on what makes you unique and start building your quick cash blueprint today.

Choosing the Right Online Platform

Choosing the right online platform is crucial when it comes to building a successful online business or side hustle. With countless options available, it can be overwhelming to determine which platform will best suit your needs and goals. In this subchapter, we will explore some key factors to consider when selecting the right online platform for your quick cash endeavors.

Understanding the behavioral tendencies and preferences of your intended market is a critical foundational action when developing a compelling and successful online presence.

It is crucial to delve deeply into not only the virtual spaces frequented by your audience but also to closely examine their online behaviors, engagement habits, and the favored methods they employ to communicate and interact.

This level of insight enables you to tailor your digital offerings and interactions to closely match what your audience finds relevant and engaging.

Additionally, gaining a thorough comprehension of the content and platforms that resonate most with your target demographic allows you to craft strategies that align with their online consumption patterns.

Such a strategic approach in identifying where your audience spends their time, the kind of content that captivates their attention, and the ways they prefer to connect, lays a solid foundation for establishing a robust, relevant, and interactive online presence, thus greatly enhancing the chances of your success in the digital realm.

Are they scrolling through Facebook, curating Pinterest boards, or joining conversations on Twitter? Perhaps they're keen shoppers, frequently browsing through the virtual aisles of Amazon or exploring unique handmade goods on Etsy.

Your audience may indeed show a greater level of active participation within professional spaces such as LinkedIn, or they might gravitate towards specialized forums that cater to niche concerns and unique hobbies.

Being attuned to these subtleties is instrumental in unraveling where your audience dedicates their attention and energy.

A comprehensive grasp of these preferences informs and influences your strategic decisions regarding which online platforms are most advantageous for your business to establish a presence on.

It can steer your choice toward particular social networks, professional sites, or niche-specific online communities. This level of understanding underpins not just the choice of platform but also shapes the kind of content you produce and the tone of your engagement, enhancing your ability to connect effectively with your audience and fostering an online environment where your brand can thrive.

Recognizing and responding to these detailed audience characteristics is essential for optimizing your digital marketing efforts and making informed, impactful decisions about your online business activities.

Selecting the right digital environment ensures that your marketing efforts resonate and your products or services are positioned right where your potential customers are most attentive, thereby increasing the effectiveness of your reach and amplifying your online impact.

As you venture further into the realm of online business, it's imperative to examine the suite of features and resources provided by various digital platforms meticulously. Many platforms equip you with comprehensive marketing tools, in-depth analytics to track your progress, and dedicated customer service teams to assist with any issues.

Conversely, it is crucial to note that not all platforms come equipped with built-in resources for marketing, comprehensive data analysis, and robust user support. In these cases, the onus falls directly upon you as the business owner to skillfully manage these facets.

This includes creating and executing your own marketing campaigns, meticulously analyzing data to inform business decisions, and developing a responsive support system for your users.

Such self-sufficiency demands a high degree of initiative and competence, underscoring the importance of reflecting deeply on which platform features and functionalities are indispensable for the seamless functioning and expansion of your enterprise.

Before committing to a platform, take the time to critically assess your own capacity to handle these essential tasks and consider the impact of potentially not having these tools at your disposal. Evaluate which platform capabilities are non-negotiable for your business's operation and future scalability.

Your decision should align with your business needs, technical proficiency, and the resources you are willing to invest in building a constructive environment that fosters sustained growth and customer satisfaction.

Selecting the right platform—a decision informed by thoughtful consideration of these elements—will serve as a solid foundation for your business's online activity.

Whether it's the ease of integrated promotion capabilities, the clarity offered by analytics, or the convenience of having accessible customer care, prioritizing these aspects is crucial.

Opt for a platform that not only meets your immediate requirements but also supports your long-term business objectives and harmonizes with the vision you have for your online venture.

Additionally, think about the scalability of the platform. As your business grows, you may need more advanced features or the ability to handle a larger volume of transactions. Choose a platform that can grow with you and accommodate your evolving needs.

The quest for the perfect online platform for your business is a highly personalized endeavor, contingent upon a trifecta of fundamental factors: your specific business objectives, the particular characteristics and behaviors of your target audience, and the financial resources you have allocated for this purpose.

It is imperative to undertake thorough research and meticulous comparison among the diverse array of platforms available.

This diligent scrutiny will enable you to discern the platform that not only accommodates your unique needs but also supports your ambitions of unleashing swift online profits and steering you towards the ultimate prize of financial autonomy.

Dedicate time to explore each potential platform's feature set, fee structures, audience reach, and integration capabilities to ensure it aligns with your business model.

Consider seeking advice from industry peers, attending webinars, and utilizing trial periods to comprehensively understand the advantages and limitations of each option.

Engaging in a comprehensive analysis of your business needs in comparison with the features and capabilities of various online platforms enables you to reach a well-rounded and informed conclusion.

Such a decision creates a solid base for your digital ventures, laying the groundwork for a stable and productive online presence. A judicious choice in platform supports the rapid development and growth of your online business pursuits and serves as a catalyst that moves you more swiftly towards a prosperous digital enterprise.

As you meticulously match platform offerings to your unique set of requirements, you strengthen your trajectory towards not just a thriving online marketplace, but also towards the greater goal of financial self-reliance.

This process is invaluable, as it ensures that your investment in digital infrastructure is attuned to both your immediate operational needs and your long-term strategic ambitions, effectively fueling your journey towards economic independence.

By choosing the right platform, you can set yourself up for success and maximize your earning potential.

Establishing Realistic Goals for Quick Cash Generation

The pursuit of fast financial returns is an enticing endeavor, and within this subchapter, we take a comprehensive look at the imperative of setting pragmatic objectives to guide this quest.

For driven entrepreneurs, those yearning for entrepreneurship, dedicated parents managing home life, diligent students, individuals pursuing side projects, and those on the pathway to financial sovereignty, crafting attainable milestones is paramount.

This practice of goal-setting transcends mere planning; it serves as a beacon, providing direction and clarity amidst the bustling internet marketplace. Establishing clear, measurable, and time-bound goals anchors your aspirations, allowing you to devise a structured action plan.

Setting clear benchmarks serves as a vital toolkit, providing you with discernible milestones that act as motivators, keeping your enthusiasm high and your resolve unwavering as you advance in your quest for rapid and noteworthy online earnings.

These benchmarks are not just waypoints marking the route; they play a critical role in evaluating your achievements and enabling a strategic reassessment of methods whenever obstacles arise in the pursuit of digital wealth.

They furnish a structured approach to tracking your journey, offering concrete instances of success to celebrate and reflect upon. Moreover, they provide a framework for constructive reflection, allowing you to realign your strategies and optimize your tactics to navigate the intricate terrain of generating revenue online.

In doing so, these benchmarks become instrumental in both charting your course and serving as tools for continuous improvement on the path to digital financial success.

When it comes to making quick cash online, it can be easy to get caught up in the excitement of the possibilities. However, without clear and realistic goals, it is easy to lose sight of what you are trying to achieve.

By establishing goals that are specific, measurable, attainable, relevant, and time-bound (SMART), you can ensure that you are on the right track to generating quick cash in a sustainable manner.

Strategically setting attainable objectives for swift cash generation demands a thorough examination of your present financial landscape. It's critical to comprehensively assess your existing fiscal condition and pinpoint the exact amount of income necessary to reach your financial aspirations.

This entails rigorously cataloging your current financial resources, understanding your expenses, and establishing the income required to meet or exceed your living standards or savings targets.

Armed with this knowledge, you can define clear, quantifiable goals that not only reflect your immediate monetary needs but also align with your broader financial ambitions.

A precise understanding of these financial parameters ensures that the targets you set for generating quick cash are both practical and meaningful, paving a confident path toward achieving your envisioned economic milestones and bolstering your overall financial well-being.

By breaking down your financial goals into smaller, manageable steps, you can create a roadmap that will guide you towards success.

Moreover, maintaining a level of flexibility is crucial when striving for success in the variable terrain of the online marketplace. The digital economy is known for its rapid fluctuations and innovations, meaning that strategies that deliver results today might not hold their efficacy in the future.

It's essential to remain nimble and receptive to altering your goals as the digital landscape shifts. By cultivating this adaptability and staying alert to emerging trends and potential opportunities, you enhance your ability to stay ahead of the curve.

Staying adaptable ensures that you're prepared to pivot your approach and embrace fresh strategies to continue generating quick cash despite the ever-changing, swift-paced nature of the online environment.

Embracing this flexible mindset is a key component to not only navigating but flourishing within the online marketplace, and it can significantly amplify your likelihood of ongoing financial success.

Ultimately, by establishing realistic goals for quick cash generation, you can set yourself up for success and build a solid foundation for rapid online earnings.

Stay focused, stay motivated, and keep pushing towards your financial independence goals.

Chapter 3: Strategies for Rapid Online Earnings

Leveraging Affiliate Marketing for Quick Cash

In today's digital age, affiliate marketing has emerged as a powerful tool for individuals looking to generate quick cash online. Leveraging affiliate marketing can be a game-changer for entrepreneurs and aspiring entrepreneurs, stay-at-home parents, students, side hustlers, and financial independence seekers.

With the right strategies and dedication, anyone can tap into the potential of affiliate marketing to create a steady stream of passive income.

Affiliate marketing embodies a business strategy wherein you promote products or services provided by external vendors or companies. In this role, you effectively become a brand champion, using various marketing techniques to recommend these offerings to your audience.

When your efforts lead to transactions or qualified leads generated through the unique affiliate hyperlink assigned to you, financial compensation in the form of commission-based earnings becomes your prize.

This passive income stream can be quite lucrative, as it provides monetary gains not necessarily tied to your own product inventory or service delivery. It hinges on your ability to successfully connect sellers with buyers within your network, turning your advocacy into potential profit.

By leveraging your marketing acumen and audience influence, you create a valuable partnership between the companies you represent and consumers, benefiting from each conversion your promotional endeavors help to manifest.

The appeal of affiliate marketing as a business model lies largely in its accessibility; it boasts a low barrier to entry, often requiring little to no upfront investment, making it an attractive option for budding entrepreneurs.

This approach allows individuals to begin their marketing efforts without the burden of significant initial expenses, providing a path to entrepreneurship that is comparatively low-risk.

Additionally, the inherent flexibility and scalability of affiliate marketing mean that it can be expanded and adjusted quickly in response to market trends, affiliate performance, and growth strategies, presenting a potentially profitable trajectory for those who navigate it successfully.

With the right marketing strategies and audience engagement, an affiliate marketing endeavor can go from a side project to a primary revenue stream. The model's adaptability ensures that it remains relevant across various niches and customer bases, allowing marketers to tap into different markets as opportunities arise.

This versatility and potential for rapid expansion contribute to its status as a compelling business model with promising prospects for growth and financial return.

Such scalability makes it a particularly appealing option for both newcomers and seasoned digital marketers who aim to bolster their online earning potential.

Its effectiveness is enhanced when paired with smart marketing strategies and a keen understanding of your audience, solidifying affiliate marketing as a prime choice for anyone intent on crafting a robust online revenue stream.

To leverage affiliate marketing for quick cash, it's essential to choose the right affiliate programs that align with your niche and target audience. Researching and selecting high-quality products or services that you believe in will help build trust with your audience and increase your chances of making sales.

At the heart of thriving affiliate marketing lies the creation of enticing, high-quality content that not only captivates but also educates and solves the unique problems faced by your intended audience.

Whether you're crafting deeply informative blog posts, curating bustling social media content, developing finely-tuned email marketing campaigns, or producing captivating videos, the success of these content pieces is crucial.

Their ability to resonate with viewers and readers is what will ideally draw them towards engaging with your affiliate links. Content of this caliber acts as a magnet for potential customers, drawing them in through its relevance and value.

It's through this compelling content that trust is built, which in turn fosters a connection that motivates your audience to act on your recommendations.

As such, the strength and appeal of your content are of utmost importance; they serve as the persuasive force that entices visitors to explore the products or services you endorse and, ultimately, to make purchasing decisions that lead to commission-earning conversions for you.

By consistently delivering rich, relevant material that resonates with your audience, you not only draw traffic to your digital doorstep but also bolster your reputation as a credible and trusted expert in your field.

This elevated status as an authority amplifies the impact of your recommendations and can significantly boost your affiliate commission potential.

Through a commitment to quality content that captivates and provides tangible benefits, you catalyze a virtuous cycle of trust and value, fostering a loyal following more inclined to respond positively to your affiliate endorsements.

Achieving success in affiliate marketing is intimately tied to the consistent use of proven strategies and a dedication to continuous improvement in your advertising and promotional endeavors.

By adopting industry best practices and relentlessly tweaking and perfecting your techniques, you position yourself to tap into faster streams of online revenue.

This effort not only involves understanding what attracts and retains an audience but also means keeping abreast of marketing trends, leveraging analytical data to guide your actions, and adapting to changes in consumer behavior.

As you refine your approach and remain committed to adapting these strategic methods, you incrementally enhance your ability to effectively promote products and convert leads into sales, thereby generating a steady and increasing flow of income.

Such diligence and adaptability are critical to carving out a profitable niche in the competitive affiliate marketing landscape and laying the foundation for achieving the sought-after goal of financial independence.

This is not a journey for the faint-hearted; it demands resolute dedication, unwavering perseverance, and an eagerness to absorb new knowledge and adjust tactics in response to evolving market trends.

Yet, for those prepared to invest this level of effort and focus, affiliate marketing can transform into a highly rewarding revenue channel.

This dynamic field provides ample opportunity for those who persist, offering a potent means of reaching and surpassing your economic aspirations, allowing you to craft a sustainable and prosperous financial future.

Creating Profitable Digital Products

Creating profitable digital products can be a game-changer for anyone looking to make quick cash online. In today's digital world, there are countless opportunities to create and sell digital products that can generate passive income streams.

Whether you're an entrepreneur, stay-at-home parent, student, side hustler, or simply seeking financial independence, creating digital products can be a lucrative venture.

Developing online courses or e-books ranks among the most favored methods for generating profitable digital assets.

This approach is particularly appealing since these products require only a one-time effort to create but can be sold an infinite number of times, potentially providing a source of passive income that can accumulate even while you are not actively working.

As you embark on the journey of creating such digital products, it's critical to pinpoint a niche market with precision and to craft content that specifically addresses the unique challenges, desires, and curiosities of that audience.

Understanding your niche's demands allows you to tailor your digital offerings to directly resonate with them, enhancing the chances that they will be willing to invest in your products.

By concentrating on delivering value in areas where there is a clear demand but potentially limited supply, your e-books and online courses stand to not just meet but exceed the expectations of your customers, thereby establishing your reputation as a reliable and authoritative source in your chosen niche.

This specificity and focus are what set apart successful digital creations, driving their ongoing sales and bolstering your income stream across various platforms.

By providing value and solving a problem for your target audience, you can increase the likelihood of your product being successful.

Delving into the realm of digital product creation, software or mobile applications stand as a particularly rewarding avenue, given the ever-growing hunger for technological innovation and convenience.

In a world that's rapidly gravitating toward technology, crafting a software product doesn't just manifest potential profits; it also provides a unique opportunity to secure a permanent foothold in the ever-expanding tech industry.

As digital reliance intensifies across all sectors, innovative software solutions that streamline processes, enhance productivity, or offer novel functionality are in high demand.

By entering the tech market with a well-designed, user-centric software product, you align yourself with the trajectory of digital advancement and position yourself to become an integral part of the technology ecosystem.

Creating software that solves real-world problems or improves everyday experiences can establish your brand as a pioneer in the tech space, leading to strong market presence and ongoing revenue streams.

As users increasingly seek out digital solutions, your software product stands as a testament to the viability of tapping into the burgeoning tech market, where quality and innovation lead to both immediate financial gains and long-term industry influence.

Your offering could range from a productivity enhancer, an immersive gaming experience, to niche-specific business applications, each catering to distinct consumer needs and interests.

The sheer diversity of potential software solutions ensures that creative and functional ideas have ample room to flourish into substantial sources of passive revenue.

Furthermore, when armed with a comprehensive strategy that encompasses robust development, astute marketing, and reliable customer support, digital products offer the prospect of continuous revenue.

These products stand to fulfill and evolve with the changing needs of a technologically adept audience, an audience that's constantly in search of innovative and streamlined technological solutions to enhance their daily digital interactions.

This potential for a sustained income stream hinges on the ability to anticipate user requirements and deliver timely updates and improvements that respond to and capitalize on market trends.

By continually refining your digital products and ensuring they remain at the forefront of tech advancements, you are positioning your offering to appeal to the modern consumer's appetite for the latest and greatest in technology.

Attention to user feedback, market analysis, and ongoing product enhancement are key components that can transform a one-time sale into a lasting source of income.

This strategic approach not only helps to retain your existing customer base but also attracts new users, thereby fostering an environment of growth and sustainability for your digital product in a competitive, fast-paced tech market.

In addition to online courses, e-books, and software products, digital art, photography, and music are also popular options for creating profitable digital products.

By leveraging your creative talents and skills, you can create and sell digital art, stock photos, or music tracks that cater to a specific audience.

To successfully develop profitable digital products, pinpointing a niche market that resonates with particular needs or interests is essential. You must tap into that niche by delivering substantial value, harnessing your unique abilities and creative flair.

Adopting a methodical strategy and utilizing effective marketing techniques are instrumental in accelerating your journey towards significant online revenue and obtaining financial self-sufficiency.

Central to this endeavor is the commitment to maintaining a laser-sharp focus, exercising relentless determination, and keeping the innovation pipeline flowing.

This relentless commitment to innovation is absolutely vital if you wish to stay ahead of the curve in the fast-moving and competitive world of digital commerce.

By constantly seeking to innovate, you ensure that your products and services are consistently aligning with the ever-changing preferences and expectations of your target market, thereby maintaining relevance in an ocean of digital alternatives.

This proactive approach to business development not only aids in distinguishing your offerings from those of your competitors but also positions you to quickly adapt to shifts in consumer behavior and industry developments.

Continuously injecting fresh ideas and enhancements into your digital commerce strategy not simply satiates the existing demands of your market but also anticipates future needs, thereby securing a loyal customer base.

Within a digital ecosystem where emerging technologies and shifting market trends have the power to overhaul established norms, the capacity to innovate emerges as your most crucial asset.

It allows you to offer significant and attractive benefits to your customers, effortlessly adapting to their evolving needs and preferences.

This relentless pursuit of innovation not only helps you in providing standout value but also strengthens your position and brand in a highly saturated market.

Enabling a consistent cycle of innovation ensures that your products, services, or content remain at the forefront of your consumers' minds, setting your business apart in a competitive and cluttered digital arena.

It's this unique proposition and commitment to reinvention that can endear your brand to customers, encourage loyalty, and secure your role as a leading figure in your industry.

By prioritizing innovation, you are not just responding to the present; you're shaping the future of your enterprise and asserting a pioneering presence that has the potential to influence the digital marketplace for years to come.

Monetizing Your Blog or Website for Quick Returns

Entrepreneurs, hopeful business starters, dedicated parents balancing caregiving with income generation, ambitious students, supplemental income enthusiasts, and those on the path to financial freedom will find that harnessing the power of content creation through a blog or website is an expedient means to achieve online profitability.

By deploying strategic measures such as targeted content marketing, search engine optimization, and affiliate partnerships, you can swiftly transform your digital presence into a revenue-generating powerhouse.

The key lies in crafting high-quality content that resonates with your audience and effectively utilizing monetization tools that complement your site's offerings.

With steadfast commitment and the meticulous implementation of a well-considered strategy, your online platform has the capacity to evolve beyond a basic hub for disseminating information.

It can grow into an invaluable financial asset, one that consistently produces income and contributes to the overall health of your economic endeavors.

By dedicating the requisite time and energy to refining your approach and staying abreast of the latest digital trends, you can enhance the value of your platform, making it a powerhouse for both knowledge and wealth creation.

Such a transformation requires not just hard work but also a vision infused with clarity and foresight. By marrying compelling content with savvy monetization tactics, nurturing audience relationships, and leveraging analytics for informed decision-making, you propel your platform into a lucrative space that serves its users while also securing a steady stream of revenue.

This journey from a simple content provider to a major commercial player in the digital realm is founded on a strategic pathway charted by your insights, expertise, and unwavering resolve to succeed.

Such an asset fortifies your fiscal ambitions, delivering financial results with expediency and exactness.

By consistently curating high-quality content, fostering meaningful engagement, and offering sought-after solutions, your platform can establish itself as an esteemed source within its niche.

This transformation from a simple conduit of information to a robust, profit-earning entity is contingent on understanding and serving your audience's needs effectively.

By aligning your offerings with market demands and leveraging the right monetization strategies, you can create a steady stream of income.

With the addition of revenue streams through your online platform, you bolster your current financial position while simultaneously constructing a robust economic base for future stability and prosperity.

This strategic development serves as a protective measure for your present-day financial targets and establishes a resilient framework for sustained financial health.

By focusing on the longevity and profitability of your platform, you are securing an asset that will flourish not just momentarily but will offer a lasting impact on your financial security.

This proactive approach to building and nurturing your platform's revenue-generating capabilities is key to creating a dependable source of income that can weather market volatility and changes in consumer behavior.

Such foresight in planning and execution ensures that you are not merely in a state of economic survival but are actively paving a way towards a future rich in financial opportunities.

It positions your online endeavors as integral components of your comprehensive financial strategy, contributing consistently to your overall wealth and economic fortitude over time.

One of the first steps to monetizing your blog or website is to identify your target audience and niche.

By understanding who your audience is and what they are interested in, you can tailor your content and offerings to better meet their needs and increase your chances of generating revenue.

Having grasped a thorough comprehension of who your target audience is, including their interests and behaviors, you are well-positioned to venture into various monetization strategies.

There are several well-established avenues for generating revenue from a blog or website, each with its own set of advantages.

Affiliate marketing allows you to earn commission by promoting other companies' products or services that align with your content and audience.

Sponsored content involves partnering with brands to create posts or articles that subtly promote their offerings, while display advertising generates income through ad placements on your site.

Additionally, you can capitalize on your expertise and audience trust by selling your own digital products—such as e-books, online courses, or software—or by offering specialized services that provide value to your visitors.

Choosing the right monetization methods will depend on the nature of your content, the preferences of your audience, and the level of engagement you maintain with your followers. Diversifying your income streams can also be effective, as it can reduce reliance on a single source and spread potential risks.

With a combination of these monetization techniques, you can transform your online platform into a multifaceted business that not only caters to the needs and interests of your audience but also contributes to your financial success.

Affiliate marketing involves promoting products or services from other companies and earning a commission for each sale or lead generated through your unique affiliate link.

Sponsored content involves partnering with brands to create content that promotes their products or services in exchange for a fee. Display advertising involves placing ads on your website and earning money based on the number of clicks or impressions.

Monetizing your blog or website becomes increasingly fruitful when you tap into the arena of digital product or service offerings, such as informative e-books, immersive online courses, or specialized consulting services.

By designing and presenting digital offerings that are both worthwhile and pertinent to the interests of your audience, you position yourself to lure in customers who see the value in investing in your specialized expertise and knowledge.

This approach to monetization not only enhances the earning capability of your online presence but also establishes your site as a trusted destination for high-quality, paid content or expert guidance, deepening your engagement with your audience and broadening your digital footprint.

In conclusion, monetizing your blog or website for quick returns requires careful planning, research, and execution.

By identifying your target audience, exploring different monetization options, and creating valuable digital products or services, you can unlock rapid online earnings and achieve financial success.

Chapter 4: Implementing the Quick Cash Code Blueprint

Developing a Consistent Content Strategy

Developing a Consistent Content Strategy is crucial for anyone looking to build a successful online business or side hustle.

In this subchapter of "The Quick Cash Code: A Blueprint for Rapid Online Earnings," we will dive into the key steps and strategies you need to implement in order to create a content plan that will drive traffic, engagement, and ultimately, revenue.

For entrepreneurs and aspiring entrepreneurs, having a consistent content strategy is essential for building brand awareness, establishing credibility, and attracting new customers.

By creating a plan that outlines what type of content you will produce, how often you will publish it, and where you will distribute it, you can ensure that your message is reaching the right audience at the right time.

Stay-at-home parents, students, and those pursuing side gigs stand to gain significantly from a well-defined content strategy. Whether your aim is to augment your household income or lay the foundation for a home-based business, establishing a structured approach to content creation and distribution is key.

Such a plan not only aids in maintaining organization and concentration but also steers you towards meeting your financial aspirations.

A disciplined content strategy can transform sporadic efforts into a cohesive framework, thereby optimizing your online engagement and ensuring your ventures are aligned with your broad economic objectives.

Financial independence seekers will find that a well-thought-out content strategy is key to unlocking rapid online earnings. By consistently producing high-quality content that resonates with your target audience, you can attract more traffic to your website, generate leads, and convert those leads into paying customers.

In this subchapter, we will cover topics such as identifying your target audience, creating a content calendar, utilizing various content formats (such as blog posts, videos, podcasts, social media posts, etc.), and measuring the success of your content strategy through analytics.

By following the tips and strategies outlined in this chapter, you will be well on your way to developing a consistent content strategy that drives results and helps you achieve your financial goals.

Building a Strong Online Presence

In today's digital age, having a strong online presence is crucial for success in any business venture. Whether you are an entrepreneur, aspiring entrepreneur, stay-at-home parent, student, side hustler, or a financial independence seeker, building a robust online presence can open up new opportunities and revenue streams.

Setting out on the path to build a strong and influential online presence begins with the crucial undertaking of establishing your brand's identity.

This initial stage requires you to design and launch an aesthetically pleasing and professionally polished website that stands as the centerpiece of your digital footprint.

In tandem, you should create and fine-tune a collection of social media profiles and other digital platforms that reflect the essence of your brand. Each of these online touchpoints must be thoughtfully developed to effectively communicate your unique value proposition and brand story to your intended audience.

This process of brand establishment involves meticulously shaping your online image and voice to resonate with your target market, ensuring consistency across all channels for maximum impact.

It's also about strategically positioning your brand in a way that differentiates you from competitors, making use of visuals, messaging, and user experience design to leave a lasting impression on visitors.

By carefully orchestrating these elements, you lay down a solid and cohesive brand identity that not only captivates your audience but also fosters recognition and loyalty, which are vital for establishing a formidable online presence.

To lay the groundwork for a thriving online presence, it's of utmost importance that every aspect of your digital footprint—from your website to your social media profiles, and any other online platforms —presents a harmonized brand image and coherent messaging.

Such consistency is instrumental in building trust and establishing credibility with potential followers and customers.

A uniform and polished brand image across all channels not only reinforces recognition but also signals professionalism and reliability, which are key in gaining the confidence of your audience.

A well-crafted and unified brand acts as the bedrock of your digital persona, anchoring your presence in the vast online arena. It is essential for forging meaningful connections with your audience, as people tend to engage more deeply with brands that exhibit authenticity and a clear sense of purpose.

Moreover, in a highly competitive digital market, a distinctive and consistent brand can distinguish your platform, setting it apart and making it memorable to consumers.

This foundational brand strategy is not only vital for initial engagement but also for long-term loyalty and success in connecting with your audience at every touchpoint in the digital journey.

Next, focus on creating valuable content that resonates with your audience. Whether it's blog posts, videos, podcasts, or social media posts, providing valuable and relevant content will help you attract and retain followers.

Engage with your audience regularly by responding to comments and messages, and participating in online conversations to build relationships and grow your network.

Invest in search engine optimization (SEO) to improve your website's visibility in search engine results. This will drive organic traffic to your website and increase your online presence.

Utilize social media marketing, email marketing, and other digital marketing strategies to reach a wider audience and drive traffic to your website.

Networking plays an indispensable role in amplifying your online presence. It's crucial to actively engage with fellow entrepreneurs, influencers, and thought leaders within your industry to broaden your exposure and forge strategic alliances.

By reaching out to these key players, you not only gain visibility but also open doors to valuable collaborations.

Working together with others in your niche can be incredibly beneficial, enabling you to tap into their follower base, exchange insights, and often create content that is mutually beneficial.

These partnerships and connections can dramatically accelerate the growth of your online persona. By associating with established figures and leveraging their credibility, you can significantly amplify your impact.

Shared ventures, such as joint webinars, co-authored content, or social media cross-promotion, can introduce you to a wider audience much more rapidly than solo efforts.

Through networking, you not only expand your reach but also enhance your reputation by affiliation, demonstrating your active participation in the community and commitment to delivering value.

This proactive approach to building relationships is a powerful catalyst for developing a robust and influential online platform.

By following these strategies and consistently working on building your online presence, you can unlock rapid online earnings and achieve financial success in today's competitive digital landscape.

Engaging with Your Target Audience for Maximum Impact

Engaging with your target audience is crucial for maximizing the impact of your online business. In "The Quick Cash Code: A Blueprint for Rapid Online Earnings," we delve into the strategies that will help you connect with your target audience in a meaningful way.

For entrepreneurs and those aspiring to etch their digital success stories, active engagement with your target audience is a cornerstone of growth.

Delving into their unique needs, discerning their preferences, and empathizing with their challenges empowers you to customize your offerings, crafting products or services that address their exact expectations.

Gaining a nuanced comprehension of your target audience is imperative - it enables you to customize your products, services, and marketing efforts to meet their unique needs and preferences effectively. Such a refined approach goes beyond simply attracting an audience; it fosters the development of a dedicated customer base that feels understood and valued.

This deep connection with customers is at the heart of building a long-lasting relationship with them and is a critical driver behind cultivating brand loyalty. This level of attunement and custom-tailoring to your audience doesn't just attract a once-off purchase; it helps create an ecosystem where customers return time and again.

By prioritizing and achieving high levels of customer satisfaction, you build a solid groundwork for a business model that is resilient and capable of sustaining itself over the long term. Happy, satisfied customers become the lifeblood of the venture, often acting as brand advocates and contributing to organic growth through word-of-mouth recommendations.

It's this cyclical dynamic of understanding, satisfying, and delighting your customers that anchors a thriving, customer-centered business poised for success.

Loyalty from such customer relationships often translates into continued patronage and word-of-mouth recommendations, further solidifying your market presence and enhancing your brand's reach.

The result is a virtuous cycle of business growth, retention, and profitability that is powered by the valuable connections made through genuine audience engagement.

Stay-at-home parents, students, and side hustlers can also benefit from engaging with their target audience. By creating content that resonates with their audience and addressing their concerns, they can attract more followers and potential customers.

This can lead to increased sales and revenue, helping them achieve their financial goals.

For financial independence seekers, engaging with the target audience is essential for building a sustainable online income stream. By consistently providing value to their audience through blogs, social media posts, or email newsletters, they can establish themselves as thought leaders in their niche.

This can lead to more opportunities for partnerships, collaborations, and sponsorships, further boosting their income potential.

In "The Quick Cash Code," we provide practical tips and strategies for engaging with your target audience effectively. From conducting market research to creating compelling content, we guide you through the process of building a strong connection with your audience for maximum impact.

By implementing these strategies, you can unlock rapid online earnings and achieve financial success in no time.

Chapter 5: Scaling Your Quick Cash Business

Outsourcing and Automation for Efficiency

In today's fast-paced digital world, outsourcing and automation are two key strategies that can significantly boost efficiency and productivity for entrepreneurs looking to maximize their online earnings. Whether you're a stay-at-home parent juggling multiple responsibilities, a student trying to make ends meet, or a side hustler looking to achieve financial independence, understanding how to leverage outsourcing and automation can be a game-changer for your online business.

Outsourcing tasks to freelancers or virtual assistants can free up your time to focus on high-value activities that directly impact your bottom line. By delegating routine or time-consuming tasks such as content creation, social media management, customer service, or administrative work, you can streamline your workflow and scale your business more effectively.

This allows you to work smarter, not harder, and concentrate on revenue-generating activities that drive rapid online earnings.

In the fast-paced digital landscape, leveraging automation tools and software becomes a game-changer, significantly boosting your business efficiency and operational effectiveness.

Varied technologies exist, ranging from sophisticated email marketing automation platforms that nurture customer relations to advanced social media scheduling tools that maintain your online presence with consistent posting.

These digital resources are invaluable in refining the workflow of your business, affording you the luxury to conserve time and amplify your outreach endeavors with comparably less manual input.

Delegating the routine and time-consuming tasks to reliable automation systems can free up valuable time, precious hours which can then be redirected towards the strategic planning and creative initiatives that are vital to your business's growth—elements that necessitate a personal, human touch and have the power to significantly impact your venture's success in the competitive digital marketplace.

The adoption of smart automation is more than a mere boost to productivity; it is a catalyst that speeds up your journey to not just meet but exceed your online business objectives, ensuring that every effort is aligned with your long-term vision for success.

In "The Quick Cash Code: A Blueprint for Rapid Online Earnings," we dive deep into the practical strategies and tools you can use to outsource and automate your online business for maximum efficiency.

Whether you're a seasoned entrepreneur or just starting out, mastering these principles can propel you towards your financial goals and unlock new opportunities for growth and success. Get ready to revolutionize your approach to online earnings and take your business to the next level with outsourcing and automation.

Diversifying Your Income Streams

In the digital age, it's more important than ever to diversify your income streams to secure your financial future. In this subchapter, we will explore different ways you can expand your earning potential and create multiple streams of income using the Quick Cash Blueprint for rapid online earnings.

As an entrepreneur or aspiring entrepreneur, diversifying your income streams can provide stability and security in an ever-changing market. By leveraging various online platforms and business models, you can maximize your earning potential and reach a wider audience.

For stay-at-home parents, students, and side hustlers, diversifying your income streams can provide the flexibility to work on your own terms and generate additional income to support your lifestyle. Whether you're looking to supplement your current income or transition to full-time entrepreneurship, having multiple streams of income can help you achieve your financial goals.

Financial independence seekers understand the importance of building passive income streams to achieve their long-term financial goals. By investing in different income-generating opportunities, you can create a diversified portfolio that generates consistent cash flow and helps you build wealth over time.

In this subchapter, we will explore various ways to diversify your income streams, including affiliate marketing, e-commerce, freelancing, online courses, and more. By combining different strategies and leveraging the power of the internet, you can unlock new opportunities for rapid online earnings and achieve financial success.

Whether you're looking to supplement your income, start a new business, or achieve financial independence, diversifying your income streams is key to maximizing your earning potential and securing your financial future. Stay tuned as we dive deeper into the Quick Cash Code and discover how you can unlock rapid online earnings through a variety of income-generating opportunities.

Investing Your Quick Cash Profits for Long-Term Growth

In the world of rapid online earnings, it's easy to get caught up in the excitement of making quick cash. However, for long-term success and financial growth, it's important to invest your quick cash profits wisely. By strategically investing your earnings, you can set yourself up for sustainable growth and financial independence in the future.

A pivotal approach for capitalizing on the quick cash earnings and securing enduring financial expansion is to implement diversification in your investment portfolio.

Embracing this strategy involves the judicious allocation of funds across an eclectic mix of asset classes, including but not limited to equities, fixed income instruments like bonds, tangible assets such as real estate, and an array of alternative investment opportunities.

The essence of diversification is to spread exposure and minimize the impact of volatility on your investments, thus protecting you against market unpredictability.

This methodical distribution of assets is crucial for balancing potential risk against the opportunity for appreciable returns.

By ensuring that your financial resources are not overly concentrated in any single area, you create a more resilient investment foundation capable of weathering market fluctuations and fostering sustained growth of your wealth over the long haul.

Another important consideration when investing your quick cash profits is to set clear financial goals. Whether you're saving for retirement, a new home, or simply looking to build wealth, having specific goals in mind can help guide your investment decisions and keep you on track for long-term success.

Additionally, it's important to stay informed about the latest investment trends and opportunities. By staying up to date on market developments and economic indicators, you can make informed decisions about where to put your money for the best long-term growth potential.

Achieving lasting financial growth from your quick cash profits is an exercise in strategic foresight, thorough research, and steadfast discipline.

It necessitates a thoughtful approach to investment, a keen understanding of market dynamics, and a commitment to stay the course despite the inevitable ebbs and flows of the economic landscape.

By adhering to these well-considered strategies and maintaining a clear vision of your long-term financial objectives, you are well-positioned to transition your initial quick cash influx into a robust and enduring foundation of wealth.

This diligent process helps to ensure that the earnings you generate today can evolve into a reliable pillar of financial stability and autonomy in the years to come.

Chapter 6: Overcoming Challenges and Staying Motivated

Dealing with Setbacks and Failure

Dealing with setbacks and failure is an inevitable part of any entrepreneurial journey. In the world of rapid online earnings, there will be times when things don't go as planned, strategies fail, and expectations are not met.

However, it is important to remember that setbacks and failures are not the end of the road, but rather opportunities for growth and learning.

For those on the entrepreneurial path, whether as established business owners or hopeful starters, as well as stay-at-home parents striving to contribute to their family's income, students juggling academia with financial obligations, individuals engaging in side ventures, and anyone on the quest for financial independence, cultivating resilience and an optimistic outlook is fundamental when navigating challenges.

Failure need not be a stumbling block that halts your progress; rather, it should be perceived as a valuable learning opportunity, a catalyst for growth leading you closer to your ultimate goals.

When confronted with setbacks, it's an occasion to critically evaluate and tweak your tactics, to gain insight from what didn't go as planned, and to fortify your resolve. This adaptive approach not only prepares you to rebound with increased vigor and wisdom but also equips you with the tenacity and experience necessary to forge ahead on your journey with a reinforced sense of purpose and determination.

Navigating through setbacks requires unwavering focus on your long-term aspirations, ensuring that transient defeats do not overshadow your larger ambitions. It is imperative to acknowledge that the road to success is rarely a direct route—it often winds through trials and tribulations that are a natural part of the growth process.

Embrace persistence as your guiding principle. Staying the course in the face of adversity is essential to achieving your goals. Continue to propel yourself onward with relentless drive, maintaining a steadfast commitment to your objectives, and remember the power of resiliency.

It's this tenacity and the refusal to relinquish your dreams that will ultimately steer you toward triumph, even when the journey becomes demanding and convoluted.

Another important aspect of dealing with setbacks is to seek support from mentors, peers, and online communities. Surround yourself with like-minded individuals who can offer guidance, advice, and encouragement during tough times.

By sharing your experiences and learning from others, you can gain valuable insights and perspectives that can help you navigate through challenges more effectively.

In conclusion, encountering setbacks and failures is an inevitable aspect of the entrepreneurial expedition. Cultivating resilience, fostering a positive mental attitude, and tapping into the support of mentors, peers, or a community can be pivotal in surmounting these barriers.

With persistence and the guidance provided by the Quick Cash Code blueprint, you are well-equipped to navigate through hurdles and unlock swift online revenue. It is essential to embrace each setback not as a defeat but as a fertile ground for learning and personal development, which can pave the way to greater achievements.

Recognize that every challenge is an opportunity to refine your approach, enhance your skills, and fortify your resolve, all of which are invaluable in the quest to thrive within your digital income ventures.

Staying Focused on Your Quick Cash Goals

In order to successfully achieve your quick cash goals, it is essential to stay focused and disciplined throughout the process. Distractions can easily derail your progress, so it is important to establish a clear plan and stick to it.

Here are some tips to help you stay focused on your quick cash goals:

1. Set Specific and Achievable Goals: Clearly define your quick cash goals and break them down into smaller, manageable tasks. This will help you stay on track and measure your progress along the way.

2. Create a Daily Action Plan: Develop a daily routine that prioritizes tasks related to your quick cash goals. Set aside specific time each day to work towards achieving them, whether it's creating content, marketing your products, or reaching out to potential clients.

3. Eliminate Distractions: Identify any distractions that may hinder your progress and find ways to eliminate or minimize them. This could include turning off notifications on your phone, setting specific work hours, or creating a designated workspace free from distractions.

4. Stay Motivated: Keep yourself motivated by reminding yourself of the reasons why you set your quick cash goals in the first place. Visualize the end result and the impact it will have on your life, whether it's achieving financial independence, starting a new business, or simply earning extra income.

5. Celebrate Small Wins: Acknowledge and celebrate your progress along the way, no matter how small. This will help boost your confidence and motivation to continue working towards your quick cash goals.

By staying focused and committed to your quick cash goals, you can turn your dreams into reality and unlock rapid online earnings. Remember to stay disciplined, eliminate distractions, and celebrate your achievements to keep yourself on track towards success.

Celebrating Your Successes and Milestones

In the fast-paced world of online entrepreneurship, it can be easy to get caught up in the daily grind of chasing after success. However, it is equally important to take a step back and celebrate your wins along the way.

Recognizing and acknowledging your successes and milestones not only boosts your morale but also motivates you to keep pushing forward towards your financial goals.

As an entrepreneur or aspiring entrepreneur, stay-at-home parent, student, side hustler, or financial independence seeker, celebrating your successes is crucial for maintaining a positive mindset and staying motivated on your journey to rapid online earnings.

Whether you have just landed your first client, hit a revenue milestone, or achieved a personal goal, taking the time to acknowledge your achievements can help you stay focused and energized.

One way to celebrate your successes is to set aside time each week to reflect on your accomplishments. This could be as simple as writing down your wins in a journal or sharing them with a friend or mentor.

You could also treat yourself to a small reward, such as a nice dinner or a relaxing day off, to commemorate your achievements.

Another important aspect of celebrating your successes is sharing them with others.

By sharing your wins with your peers, you not only inspire and motivate them but also build a supportive network of like-minded individuals who can cheer you on during both the highs and lows of your entrepreneurial journey.

Remember, every success, no matter how small, is a stepping stone towards your ultimate goal of financial freedom. So take the time to celebrate your successes and milestones, no matter how big or small, and keep pushing forward on your quick cash blueprint to unlock rapid online earnings.

Chapter 7: The Quick Cash Code Success Stories

Entrepreneur Success Stories

In this subchapter, we will delve into the inspiring stories of successful entrepreneurs who have utilized the Quick Cash Blueprint to achieve rapid online earnings. These stories serve as a testament to the effectiveness of the strategies outlined in this book and can provide valuable insights and motivation for entrepreneurs and aspiring entrepreneurs alike.

One inspiring example of entrepreneurial triumph comes from Sarah, a stay-at-home mom who sought a flexible solution to boost her family's income without sacrificing precious moments with her children. By embracing the Quick Cash Blueprint as her guide, Sarah ventured into the world of e-commerce and launched an online store focused on selling her unique handmade crafts.

Her initial efforts soon blossomed into a burgeoning business thanks to her unwavering dedication and diligent work ethic. Through careful planning and relentless effort,

Sarah not only achieved financial independence but also successfully established a stable and lasting source of income that supports her family's needs and aspirations.

Her story serves as a beacon to others showing that with commitment and the right strategies, balancing family life with financial growth is genuinely attainable.

Mark's journey adds another layer of inspiration, showcasing how strategic planning can yield substantial results.

As a college student burdened with the rising costs of tuition, Mark turned to the techniques and strategies delineated within the Quick Cash Blueprint to carve out a new financial path. He cleverly leveraged his academic strengths to establish a thriving online tutoring enterprise.

This venture did more than just provide a steady stream of income to offset educational expenses; it also presented him with an invaluable opportunity to deepen his expertise in his chosen area of study.

Through his entrepreneurial spirit and the application of well-defined guidelines, Mark not only managed to support his academic pursuits financially but also enhanced his professional skill set, positioning himself for future success in his field.

These success stories highlight the versatility and effectiveness of the Quick Cash Blueprint in helping individuals from all walks of life achieve their financial goals.

Whether you are a stay-at-home parent, a student, a side hustler, or simply someone seeking financial independence, the stories shared in this subchapter are sure to inspire and motivate you on your own entrepreneurial journey. Remember, with the right mindset and the right tools, success is within reach for anyone willing to put in the effort.

Stay-at-Home Parent Success Stories

In this subchapter, we will delve into the inspiring success stories of stay-at-home parents who have found financial success through the quick cash blueprint outlined in this book.

These stories serve as a testament to the power of determination, resourcefulness, and the endless possibilities that come with earning money online.

One such success story is that of Sarah, a stay-at-home mom of three who was looking for ways to supplement her family's income while still being able to care for her children full-time. Sarah stumbled upon the quick cash blueprint and decided to give it a try.

Within a few months, she was able to generate a steady stream of income through online freelancing, affiliate marketing, and selling digital products. Sarah's success not only provided her family with much-needed financial stability but also gave her a sense of empowerment and independence.

Another inspiring story is that of Mark, a stay-at-home dad who had always dreamt of starting his own online business but never knew where to begin. After reading the quick cash blueprint, Mark decided to take the plunge and launch his own e-commerce store selling handmade products.

With dedication and hard work, Mark was able to turn his passion into a profitable business that now supports his family and allows him to work on his own terms.

These success stories represent only a small sampling of the boundless potential that exists for stay-at-home parents ready to bet on their abilities and aspirations.

This book's tested and proven strategies serve as a roadmap not only for entrepreneurs and those with entrepreneurial ambitions but also for stay-at-home parents, academically engaged students, individuals pursuing additional income streams, and anyone seeking the sovereignty of financial independence.

By applying the insights and methods detailed throughout these pages, a multitude of individuals can ignite their journey toward swift online profitability and realize the financial liberation they yearn for.

Encouraging tales like these demonstrate the vastness of opportunity in the digital sphere, awaiting those with the courage and determination to seize them and craft their own narratives of success.

Student Success Stories

In this subchapter, "Student Success Stories," we delve into the inspiring journeys of students who have used The Quick Cash Code to achieve their financial goals while balancing their academic responsibilities.

These success stories serve as a testament to the effectiveness of our blueprint for rapid online earnings, demonstrating that with dedication and the right strategies, anyone can succeed in the world of online entrepreneurship.

One such success story is that of Sarah, a college student who used The Quick Cash Code to earn a steady income while pursuing her degree.

By following the step-by-step instructions laid out in the blueprint, Sarah was able to establish a profitable online business that allowed her to cover her tuition fees and living expenses without having to rely on student loans.

Another inspiring story comes from Mike, a high school student with a passion for technology. Using the principles outlined in The Quick Cash Code, Mike launched his own online tech support service and quickly gained a loyal customer base.

Not only did this venture provide him with a source of income, but it also helped him develop valuable skills that would serve him well in his future career endeavors.

These student success stories highlight the versatility and accessibility of The Quick Cash Code for individuals from all walks of life. Whether you are a student looking to earn extra income, a stay-at-home parent seeking financial independence, or an aspiring entrepreneur with a side hustle, this blueprint can help you unlock rapid online earnings and achieve your financial goals.

So don't wait any longer — join the ranks of successful students who have found financial success with The Quick Cash Code today!

Side Hustler Success Stories

In this subchapter, we will delve into inspiring side hustler success stories that will motivate and encourage you on your own journey to financial independence.

These individuals have taken their passion, skills, and determination to create additional streams of income through various side hustles, and their stories serve as a testament to the possibilities that exist in the world of online earnings.

Sarah's tale is particularly uplifting, illustrating a scenario where creativity and enterprise collide to foster success. As a stay-at-home mom, she launched a flourishing Etsy shop, specializing in the craft of bespoke handmade jewelry. By dedicating just a handful of productive hours daily—expertly balanced with her parenting duties —Sarah created a reliable source of revenue.

This additional income not only contributed to her family's financial stability but also offered her personal satisfaction and a rewarding sense of professional achievement beyond her invaluable role as a parent.

Her story is a testament to the possibility of harnessing one's passions and skills to build a thriving home-based business that provides both monetary support and a sense of personal accomplishment.

Another inspiring tale comes from Mike, a college student who turned his love for graphic design into a profitable freelance business. By leveraging online platforms to showcase his work and connect with clients, Mike was able to earn enough money to cover his tuition and living expenses while gaining valuable real-world experience in his field.

These success stories highlight the diverse opportunities available to side hustlers in today's digital age. Whether you have a creative talent, a valuable skill, or a unique product to offer, there is immense potential for you to unlock rapid online earnings and achieve your financial goals.

By learning from the experiences of these successful side hustlers, you can gain valuable insights, tips, and strategies to help you navigate the world of online entrepreneurship and create a sustainable income stream that complements your existing work or lifestyle.

So, take inspiration from these stories, believe in your abilities, and start your own journey towards side hustler success today.

Chapter 8: Taking Action and Unlocking Your Quick Cash Potential

Creating Your Personal Quick Cash Action Plan

Securing swift online profits and attaining financial freedom hinge on the creation and execution of a detailed and purposeful action plan.

The content within this subchapter is designed to walk you through the crucial stages of devising a tailored quick cash action plan that aligns seamlessly with your individual aspirations and unique situation.

By helping you to identify clear objectives, set achievable milestones, and strategize effective pathways to meet them, this guidance aims to equip you with the tools necessary to translate your goals into tangible results.

A personalized plan ensures that you approach your financial journey with focus and precision, enabling you to navigate the path to rapid online earnings and financial autonomy with confidence.

Step 1: Define Your Financial Goals
The first step in creating your action plan is to clearly define your financial goals.

Whether you are looking to earn extra income to supplement your current job, replace your full-time income, or achieve financial independence, having a clear goal in mind will help you stay focused and motivated.

Step 2: Identify Your Strengths and Resources
Next, take stock of your strengths, skills, and resources that you can leverage to achieve your financial goals. Are you good at writing, graphic design, or social media marketing?

Do you have a network of contacts or access to certain tools or resources that can help you succeed? By identifying your strengths and resources, you can create a plan that plays to your strengths and maximizes your chances of success.

Step 3: Set Specific, Measurable, Achievable, Relevant, and Time-bound (SMART) Goals
Once you have defined your financial goals and identified your strengths and resources, it is important to set SMART goals that will guide your actions and track your progress.

For example, if your goal is to earn $1,000 per month through online freelancing, you could set a specific goal of completing five projects per month, each paying $200.

Step 4: Take Action and Stay Consistent

Finally, it is time to take action and implement your quick cash action plan. Whether you are starting a side hustle, freelancing, or launching an online business, consistency is key to achieving rapid online earnings.

Make a commitment to work on your goals daily, track your progress, and make adjustments as needed to stay on track.

Adhering to the outlined steps to craft a custom-tailored quick cash action plan paves the way for you to access accelerated online earnings and advance significantly toward your fiscal objectives.

Regardless of whether you are an established entrepreneur, a diligent stay-at-home parent looking to contribute financially, a student managing studies and financial resources, someone pursuing side hustles, or simply someone on the journey to financial self-sufficiency, this blueprint is a valuable tool.

It's designed to propel you forward, providing a structured and strategic approach for navigating the dynamic and often complex landscape of online income generation.

Deploying this compass, you'll be well-equipped to take decisive action, channel effort effectively, and position yourself for success in the bustling marketplace of online business.

Implementing the Strategies outlined in the Quick Cash Code Blueprint

The strategies outlined in the Quick Cash Code Blueprint are designed to help individuals from various walks of life generate rapid online earnings.

For entrepreneurs and aspiring entrepreneurs looking to increase their income streams, implementing these strategies can provide a quick and effective way to boost their bottom line.

By following the step-by-step instructions laid out in the blueprint, they can leverage the power of the internet to create a sustainable source of income.

Stay-at-home parents can also benefit greatly from the Quick Cash Code Blueprint. With flexible hours and the ability to work from home, this blueprint offers a practical solution for parents looking to earn extra income while still prioritizing their family responsibilities.

By following the strategies outlined in the blueprint, stay-at-home parents can tap into new revenue streams and achieve financial independence without having to sacrifice time with their loved ones.

Students and side hustlers can also find value in the Quick Cash Code Blueprint. Whether they are looking to pay off student loans, save for the future, or simply earn some extra cash on the side, this blueprint provides a roadmap for success.

By putting the strategies into action, students and side hustlers can unlock new opportunities for financial growth and stability.

Ultimately, the Quick Cash Code Blueprint is a valuable resource for anyone seeking to achieve financial independence. By implementing the strategies outlined in the blueprint, individuals can take control of their financial future and build a solid foundation for long-term success.

Whether you are an entrepreneur, stay-at-home parent, student, or side hustler, the Quick Cash Code Blueprint can help you unlock rapid online earnings and reach your financial goals.

Continuing to Learn and Adapt for Ongoing Success

In the fast-paced world of online entrepreneurship, the key to ongoing success lies in the ability to continually learn and adapt to new trends and strategies.

As outlined in "The Quick Cash Code: A Blueprint for Rapid Online Earnings," staying ahead of the curve is essential for entrepreneurs and aspiring entrepreneurs looking to maximize their online earnings.

The Quick Cash Blueprint stands as an all-encompassing manual for stay-at-home parents, industrious students, committed side hustlers, and those set on the trail to financial freedom, offering strategic insights to harness speedy online profits.

Yet, it's essential to acknowledge that merely executing the blueprint's tactics may not suffice for sustained success. Indeed, longevity in the online business sphere demands an ongoing commitment to education and an agile approach to adaptation, keeping pace with the continuous shifts and developments in digital commerce.

Staying abreast of new trends, refining your skills, and evolving your strategies are key to not just surviving but thriving in the competitive, fast-changing world of online entrepreneurship.

One of the most important ways to continue learning and adapting is to stay informed about industry trends and changes. This can involve reading industry publications, attending webinars, and networking with other entrepreneurs.

By staying up to date on the latest developments in the online business world, you can ensure that your strategies remain relevant and effective.

Maintaining a trajectory of continuous success in the digital marketplace also rests on a foundation of experimentation and innovation. The online business climate is characteristically fluid, making it imperative for entrepreneurs to remain flexible and responsive.

Today's effective strategies may become obsolete with the tide of technological advances and consumer behavior shifts. Embracing a mindset that welcomes experimentation and exploration of novel concepts is crucial to outpacing rivals and cultivating the growth of your digital earnings.

Such a proactive stance ensures that you can adeptly navigate the currents of change, capitalize on emerging trends, and adapt to the evolving digital ecosystem—all of which are critical for preserving and enhancing your position in the online business world.

In conclusion, continuing to learn and adapt is essential for ongoing success in the world of online entrepreneurship. By staying informed, experimenting with new strategies, and remaining open to new ideas, you can ensure that your online business continues to thrive.

The Quick Cash Code provides a solid foundation for rapid online earnings, but it is up to you to continue learning and adapting in order to achieve long-term success.

Conclusion: Embracing the Quick Cash Mindset for Lasting Online Earnings Success

In summing up, fostering a quick cash mindset is a pivotal ingredient for securing enduring success in the realm of online earnings. Through "The Quick Cash Code: A Blueprint for Rapid Online Earnings," we have delved into a variety of effective strategies and practical techniques tailored to aid in the pursuit of swift online cash generation.

This mindset, focused on identifying and seizing upon opportunities for quick financial wins, is beneficial across the board – whether you're steering your own entrepreneurial venture, aspiring to launch a start-up, managing household responsibilities while earning, pursuing academic goals, looking for supplementary income streams, or striving towards the ultimate goal of financial liberty.

By wholeheartedly adopting this quick cash mindset and applying the insights from this blueprint, you're laying the groundwork for a future rich in financial independence and success.

Grasping the potency of quick cash and putting into practice the array of strategies presented in this book sets the stage for you to unleash a surge of online earnings, propelling you towards your financial aims.

The pivotal factor in translating these strategies into tangible results is proactive action.

Keeping your eyes on the prize, staying single-minded in your focus, and effectively utilizing the vast array of digital tools and platforms at your disposal are paramount.

With unwavering dedication, thorough commitment, and continual persistence, it's possible to cultivate a robust source of income online.

This stream, once established, has the potential to not only thrive but also provide enduring financial support that will continue to bolster you well into the future.

Remember, success does not happen overnight. It requires hard work, determination, and a willingness to learn and adapt. By embracing the quick cash mindset, you can position yourself for success in the ever-evolving online marketplace.

Whether you are looking to supplement your income, build a full-time business, or achieve financial independence, the principles outlined in this book can guide you on your journey.

So, take the first step towards embracing the quick cash mindset today. Start implementing the strategies and techniques outlined in this book, and watch as your online earnings grow. With the right mindset and a commitment to success, you can achieve your financial goals and create the life you desire.

The Quick Cash Code: Mastering the Art of Online Earnings

Back Cover Description: Unlock the secrets to online financial success with "The Quick Cash Code: A Blueprint for Rapid Online Earnings." This book is your essential guide to developing a 'quick cash mindset,' critical for navigating the digital economy with prowess. Inside, discover a treasure trove of strategies and hands-on techniques designed to catapult you toward immediate and substantial online earnings. Whether you're an entrepreneur setting sail in new business waters, a stay-at-home parent exploring income options, a student financing an education, or simply passionate about financial freedom, this book promises to transform your approach to making money online. Embark on a journey to financial empowerment with "The Quick Cash Code," and take the first step toward a diverse and thriving online income. Your future of independence and success awaits.

www.ingramcontent.com/pod-product-compliance
Lightning Source LLC
Chambersburg PA
CBHW070802290526
45795CB00002B/600